SERMON OUTLINES

on

The
Deeper Life

The Bryant Sermon Outline Series

SERMON OUTLINES

on

The Deeper Life

compiled by

Al Bryant

kregel
PUBLICATIONS

Grand Rapids, MI 49501

Sermon Outlines on the Deeper Life
compiled by Al Bryant

© 1992 by Kregel Publications

Published by Kregel Publications, a division of Kregel,
Inc., P.O. Box 2607, Grand Rapids, MI 49501. Kregel
Publications provides trusted, biblical publications for
Christian growth and service. Your comments and sugges-
tions are valued.

For more information about Kregel Publications, visit our
web site at: www.kregel.com

Cover design: Frank Gutbrod

Library of Congress Cataloging-in-Publication
Sermon outlines on the deeper life / compiled by Al Bryant.
          p.   cm.
1. Sermons—Outlines, syllabi, etc. I. Bryant, Al. II. Title.
BV4223.B764   1992   91-39391
251'.02—dc20

ISBN 0-8254-2053-9

2 3 4 5 / 04

Printed in the United States of America

CONTENTS

FOREWORD

The "deeper things" of the faith are often neglected in our present-day hectic lifestyle. It is to supply a resource of sermons to nourish the inner person of the heart that this selection of sermon outlines is offered to preachers and teachers everywhere. Based on Scripture passages from both the Old and New Testaments, they emphasize the importance of feeding the spiritual nature of God's people. As they are strengthened spiritually, they will be able to win in the battle of life. These outlines fulfill the admonition of Paul to Timothy to " . . . continue . . . in the things which thou hast learned and hast been assured of, knowing of whom thou hast learned them; and that from a child thou hast known the Holy Scriptures, which are able to make thee wise unto salvation through faith which is in Christ Jesus."

An unknown poet has put the thought of the "deeper life" into these words:

We love to spread our branches,
   The root-life we neglect;
We love to shine in public,
   And human praise expect;
While in our inner chamber,
   Where creature voices cease,
We may meet God in silence,
   And breath in heaven's peace.

The secret of deep living
   Lies in the secret place,
Where, time and sense forgotten,
   We see God face to face,
Beyond mere forms and symbols,
   Beyond mere words and signs,
Where, in that hidden temple,
   The Light eternal shines.

AL BRYANT

TEXTUAL INDEX

7

RESULTS OF ABIDING IN CHRIST

I. Walking as Christ walked. "So to walk, even as He walked" (1 John 2:6).

II. Loving the brethren. "He that loveth his brother abideth in the light" (1 John 2:10).

III. Not ashamed at Christ's coming. "And not be ashamed before Him at His coming" (1 John 2:28).

IV. Not sinning. "Whosoever abideth in Him, sinneth not" (1 John 3:6).

V. The witness of the Spirit. "We know He abideth in us, by the Spirit" (1 John 3:24).

VI. Possessing the Father and Son. "He that abideth . . . he hath both the Father and Son" (2 John 9).

VII. Prayers answered. "If ye abide in Me . . . ye shall ask what ye will" (John 15:7).

VIII. Fruit-bearing. "He that abideth . . . bringeth forth much fruit" (John 15:5).   F. E. MARSH

ABUNDANCE

I. Saved in abundant grace. "Where sin *abounded*" (Rom. 5:20).

II. Blessed according to abundant mercy. "Which according to His *abundant* mercy hath begotten us again" (1 Peter 1:3).

III. Energized with abundant life. "That they might have life, and that they might have it more *abundantly*" (John 10:10).

IV. Calmed in abundant peace. "*Abundance* of peace as long as the moon endured" (Ps. 72:7).

V. Rejoiced with abundant joy. "Your joy may be more *abundant* in Christ Jesus" (Phil. 1:26).

VI. Satisfied with abundant goodness. "They shall be *abundantly* satisfied with the goodness of Thy house" (Ps. 36:8).

VII. Prayer answered in abundant manner. "Able to do exceeding *abundantly*" (Eph. 3:20).   F. E. MARSH

A GRACIOUS INVITATION

And whoseover will, let him take the water of life freely (Rev. 22:17).

The Bible not only makes known our wants, but tells us where they may be supplied. Without water our bodies perish. Without the Living Water our souls are consumed with thirst. All man's spiritual needs are met and satisfied by Christ.

I. **The Blessing—"Water."**
Water is *cleansing*. Christ cleanses from sin.
Water is *satisfying*. Christ meets our yearning after God.
Water is *beautifying* and *productive*. Christ makes us holy, beautiful, useful.

II. **The Characters Invited:**
The thirsty, "Blessed are they which do hunger and thirst after righteousness."
The whole of the race, "Whosoever will." If any go away thirsty, it is not for want of an invitation, but because they will not drink of the Water of Life.

III. **The Agency Employed:**
The *Spirit*. The Holy Spirit is continually pressing home this invitation.
The *Bride*—the *Church*. Not any particular section or sect, but the Universal Church of Christ. "All who love and serve the Lord Jesus."
This soul-satisfying Water of Life is the free gift of God. It is an inexhaustible Fountain, which can never fail. Obey the invitation. Drink, and your thirst shall be eternally quenched, your soul eternally satisfied.

SERMONS IN A NUTSHELL

A BRIGHT PROMISE

"I will never leave thee, nor forsake thee" (Heb. 13:5).

The frequency of the promise of God's unfailing presence is very marked in God's Word.

I. The *Promiser* of this promise—Jehovah (Gen. 28:15).

II. The *ground* of this promise—covenant (Deut. 4:31).

III. The *power* of this promise in conflict (Deut. 31:6).

IV. The *suitability* of this promise for special work (Deut. 31:8).

V. The *certainty* of this promise (Joshua 1:5).

VI. The *reason* of the fulfillment of this promise (1 Sam. 12:22).

VII. The *stimulus* of this promise (1 Chron. 28:20).

VIII. The *condition* to be fulfilled to know the truth of this promise (1 Kings 6:12,13).

IX. The *presentness, perfectness*, and *perpetuity* of this promise (Ps. 37:28-33).

X. This promise is *valid*, although saints may not always realize it (Ps. 94:14).

XI. The *class of people* that appreciate this promise (Isa. 41:17).

XII. The *immutability* of this promise (Heb. 13:5,6).

F. E. MARSH

THE BELIEVER'S PRESENT STATE

A Possessor of Christ Life (Col. 3:3)
Partaker of a Divine Nature (2 Peter 1:4)
Indwelt by the Holy Spirit (1 Cor. 6:19)
The New Life in a Mortal Body (2 Cor. 4:10)
Groaning for Deliverance (Rom. 8:23)
Desiring to be Clothed in a New Body (2 Cor. 5:2)

JOHN RITCHIE

AMBASSADORS FOR CHRIST

Now then we are ambassadors for Christ . . . (2 Cor. 5:20).

God was in Christ reconciling the world to Himself, and Christ is in believers continuing this work of reconciliation. Study the following suggestions growing out of this subject and text.

I. The Presence of Christ Comforts Us

We believe in Christ, accept Him, confess Him as Savior and Lord. We are then ready to enter into His service of reconciling others to the Father through Christ. It is a comfort to know that Christ will go with us. "Lo, I am with you always."

II. The Purpose of Christ Constrains Us

His purpose is to save the lost people of the earth. If we love Him we will have the same desire. His love and purpose constrain us.

III. The Program of Christ Challenges Us

The program of Christ extends to the full salvation of all the people of all nations of all the earth. It is the largest task known to men. It is great enough for the most ambitious.

IV. The Person of Christ Compels Us

He stands by our side. He looks on when we do His will. He inspires us to do our best. We see Him and feel compelled to do our best for Him. It is like the son when father looks on to assist.

V. The Power of Christ Completes Us

Without Christ we can do nothing. In His strength we can do all things. We can be complete in Him. His power is available. Use it.

SERMONS IN OUTLINE
JEROME O. WILLIAMS

BELIEVERS BELONG TO CHRIST

I. "Ye are not your own, for ye are bought with a price" (1 Cor. 6:20).
   A. His purchased possession (Eph. 1:14).
   B. His redeemed (1 Peter 18:19).
   C. His peculiar treasure (Mal. 3:17, R.V.).
   D. His temple, of which He is the chief cornerstone (Eph. 2:20-22).
   E. His Church, of which He is the Head (Eph. 5:23).

II. "Members of His body, and of His flesh and of His bones" (Eph. 5:30).

III. "Quickened together with Him; raised up together with Him; sealed together with Him" (Eph. 2:5,6).

IV. "Because ye belong to Christ" (Mark 9:41).
   A. "Beloved . . . be diligent, that ye may be found in Him in peace, without spot, and blameless" (2 Peter 3:14).

TWELVE BASKETS FULL

REASONS FOR NOT FEARING

He Redeems me (Isa. 43:1).
He Protects me (Gen. 15:1).
He Strengthens me (Isa. 35:4).
He Is with me (Isa. 41:10).
He Helps me (Isa. 41:13).
He Cares for me (Matt. 10:31).
He has a Kingdom for me (Luke 12:32).

PEGS FOR PREACHERS

THE BELIEVER'S SECRET OF POWER

*Then came the disciples to Jesus apart, and said, Why could
not we cast him out? And Jesus said unto them, Because
of your unbelief (Matt. 17:19,20).*

We have success enough in Christian work to assure us that we
possess a treasure, and failures enough to make us feel how weak
are the earthen vessels that hold it.

I.   We Have an Unvarying Power.
  A.   We have a Gospel that can never grow old.
  B.   We have an abiding Spirit.
  C.   We have a Lord the same yesterday, today, and forever.

II.   The Condition of Exercising This Power Is Faith.
  With such a force at our command, a force that could shake
the mountains and break the rocks, how can we think of failure?
Christ throws the disciples back decisively upon themselves as solely
responsible.

  We have received all spiritual gifts in proportion to our
capacity, and our capacity is mainly settled by our faith. The same
faith has a natural operation upon ourselves which tends to fit us for
casting out the evil spirit. It makes us simple, fearless, strong.

  Faith has power over men who see it. There is a magnetism
in the sight of a brother's faith which few can resist.

III.   Our Faith Is Ever Threatened by Subtle Unbelief.
  Our activity in spreading the Gospel tends to become
mechanical.

  The atmosphere of scornful disbelief which surrounds us
makes our faith falter.

IV.   Our Faith Can Only Be Maintained by Constant Devotion
and Rigid Self-Denial.
  It is no holiday task to cast out devils. Self-indulgent men will
never do it.

SELECTED

THE BELIEVER'S POSITION

Given out of the world (John 17:6).
Sent into the world (John 17:18).
Left in the world (John 17:11).
Not of the world (John 17:14).
Hated by the world (John 17:14).
Kept from the evil of the world (John 17:15).

PEGS FOR PREACHERS

THE BELIEVER'S FEET

Set on a Rock (Ps. 40:2)—Salvation.
Cleansed by the Word (John 13:10)—Communion.
Kept by Divine Power (1 Sam. 2:9)—Preservation.
Shod with Peace (Eph. 6:15)—Warfare.
Running with the Gospel (Rom. 10:15)—Service.
Bruising Satan (Rom. 16:20)—Victory.

500 BIBLE SUBJECTS

THE DEVELOPMENT OF FAITH

   I. Not Faith (Mark 4:40).
  II. Little Faith (Luke 12:28).
 III. Great Faith (Matt. 8:10).
 IV. Rich Faith (James 2:5).
  V. Precious Faith (2 Peter 1:1).
 VI. Full Faith (Acts 6:5).
VII. Perfect Faith (James 2:22).

TWELVE BASKETS FULL

GOD'S PURPOSE IN CHASTENING

For Proving (Deut. 8:2-3).
For Purifying (Mal. 3:3).
For Teaching (Ps. 119:71).
For Humbling (2 Cor. 12:7).
For Restoring (Ps. 119:67).
For Promotion (Dan. 3:23, 30).

PEGS FOR PREACHERS

A SEVENFOLD VIEW OF THE LOVE OF GOD

It is Infinite in its character (John 17:23).
It is Constraining in its power (2 Cor. 5:14).
It is Inseparable in its object (Rom. 8:35-37).
It is Individual in its choice (Gal. 2:20).
It is Universal in its extent (John 3:16).
It is Unchanging in its purpose (John 8:1).
It is Everlasting in its duration (Jer. 31:3).

PEGS FOR PREACHERS

SERVANTS IN OBEDIENCE

By Nature the Servants of Sin (John 8:34)
Henceforth to Own and Serve the Lord (Acts 27:33)
Saved to Serve the Living God (1 Thess. 1:9)
Purged from Sin to Serve God (Heb. 9:14)
Obedience is the Law of Service (Rom. 6:16)
Following Christ in order to Serve (John 12:26)
The Servant's Judgment and Reward (2 Cor. 5:10)
The Eternal Service in Glory (Rev. 22:4)

JOHN RITCHIE

ETERNAL BLESSINGS OF THE BELIEVER

I. **We possess *eternal Life*.** "Whosoever believeth in Him . . . have eternal life" (John 3:15).

II. **We are secured in an *eternal Covenant*.** "Through the blood of the everlasting Covenant" (Heb. 13:20).

III. **We are saved with an *eternal Salvation*.** "He became the Author of eternal salvation" (Heb. 5:9).

IV. **We are liberated by an *eternal Redemption*.** "Having obtained eternal redemption for us" (Heb. 9:12).

V. **We have an *eternal House*.** "A house not made with hands, eternal in the heavens" (2 Cor. 5:1).

VI. **We are called to *eternal Glory*.** "Who hath called us unto His eternal glory" (1 Peter 5:10).

VII. **We are kept for an *eternal Inheritance*.** "Might receive the promise of an eternal inheritance" (Heb. 9:15).

VIII. **We are cheered by *eternal Comfort*.** "Hath given us everlasting consolation" (2 Thess. 2:16).

IX. **We know there is an *eternal Weight* of glory in the future.** "Worketh for us a far more exceeding and eternal weight of glory" (2 Cor. 4:17).

X. **We shall dwell in *eternal Tabernacles*.** "Receive you into everlasting habitations" (Luke 16:9).

XI. **We are aiming to have an abundant entrance into the *eternal Kingdom*.** "An entrance shall be ministered unto you abundantly . . . . everlasting kingdom" (2 Peter 1:11).

F. E. MARSH

THE EASY YOKE AND THE LIGHT BURDEN

For My yoke is easy, and My burden is light (Matt. 11:30).

I. The Yoke of Christ Is Easy, and His burden is light, because we bear it with the approbation of conscience. A burden which does not consist of sin is never heavy.

II. This Yoke Is Easy because it is born in love.

III. Christ's Yoke Is Easy and His burden is light because it is borne with the help of the Spirit of God.

IV. Christ's Words Are True because His burden becomes lighter the longer it is borne.

V. Christ's Yoke Is Easy and His burden light because we are sustained under it by a good hope.

• Heaven and endless happiness is reserved for us.
THREE HUNDRED OUTLINES ON THE NEW TESTAMENT

ENDURANCE IN TRIBULATION

Endure Loss in the Confession of Christ (Heb. 10:32)
Endure Hardness as a Soldier on Service (2 Tim. 2:3)
Endure Affliction as a Servant and Witness (2 Tim. 4:5)
Endure Grief in the Path of Obedience (1 Peter 2:19)
Endure Trial in the Day of Testing (James 1:12)
JOHN RITCHIE

STRENGTH FOR SERVICE

Strong in the Grace that is in Christ (2 Tim. 2:1)—To Endure
Strong in the Lord and His Power (Eph. 6:10)—To Resist
Strong in the Might of the Spirit (Eph. 3:16)—To Comprehend
Strong in the Faith in the Promises (Rom. 4:26)—To Expect
Strong, through the Word Abiding (1 John 2:14)—To Overcome
JOHN RITCHIE

THE BEST PROTECTION

*Thou wilt keep him in perfect peace, whose mind is stayed
on Thee: because he trusteth in Thee (Isa. 26:3).*

I. **The Recipient of the Promise**—The man "whose mind is
stayed."

"Mind," in margin "thought," includes imagination, idea,
desire, whole heart. "Stayed"; by deliberate act of faith shifting all
care, responsibility, result, to the One best able to take it; and being,
in consequence, left at peace from all worry.

II. **The Precious Assurance Here Given**—"Thou wilt keep
him in perfect peace."

Peace is longed for by all: individuals and nations. It is God's
gift, bestowed only on those who fulfill His conditions.

Peace, God-given, is peace at its fullest. "Perfect peace," in
the original "Peace, peace," language failing to express its fullness—
like *ff* or *pp* for music, for much loudness or much softness.

III. **The Simple, Yet Ample Reason Assigned**—"Because he
trusteth in Thee."

It is the direct outcome of faith. So simple that none can fail
to find it. "He trusteth in Thee"; ample ground for faith, for Jehovah
is the Covenant God.

The "trust" of the Old Testament is just the "faith" of the
New. Let us, therefore, who have come to God through Christ,
allow the peace of God to rule in our hearts. So shall we have peace
indeed in our hearts and homes—peace in the present, and peace
for the future.

SERMONS IN A NUTSHELL

PRACTICAL SEPARATION

From the Lusts of the Flesh (2 Tim. 2:22)
From the Lusts of the World (Titus 2:12)
From the Appearance of Evil (1 Thess. 5:22)
From the Works of Darkness (Eph. 5:11)
From the Companionship of the Ungodly (2 Cor. 6:17)

JOHN RITCHIE

BOUGHT WITH A PRICE

Ye are not your own, for ye are bought with a price:
therefore glorify God in your body, and in your spirit,
which are God's (1 Cor. 6:19,20).

How strangely this sentence sounds in the ears of human pride! With what infinite wonder does it fill the natural man!

I. **We Notice First the Great Fact Asserted in the Text, That We Are Purchased, and the Position into Which We Are Brought Because of That Purchase.**

A. We are redeemed by the precious blood of Christ, and therefore, we are not our own.

II. **What Is the Course of Conduct Which a Consideration of Such Position Will Encourage Us to Take?**

A. Let your devotedness to God be entire; glorify God in your bodies, in your intellect, in all your powers.

B. Let your devotedness be benevolent. Spend yourselves in energetic endeavors for the conversion of your fellows, and for the spread of the Gospel among you. There is an influence for good as well as an influence for evil.

C. Let your devotedness to God be consummated now— now, when the conflict between knowledge and faith, between the ceremonial and the spiritual, between the idolatrous and the ever-living, has commenced, and a thousand voices of the universe are pealing out the challenge: "Who is on the Lord's side?"

THREE HUNDRED OUTLINES ON THE NEW TESTAMENT

SUBJECTS UNDER AUTHORITY

To the Lord, as Supreme above All (Acts 5:29)
To the Father, in His Discipline of us (Heb. 12:9)
To One Another, as Fellow-saints (1 Peter 5:5)
To the Powers-that-be, in the World (Rom. 13:1)
To those who Watch for our Souls (Heb. 13:17)
Wives, unto their own Husbands (1 Peter 3:1)
Younger Saints, to the Elder (1 Peter 5:5)

JOHN RITCHIE

WHO CHRIST IS

I. He is *"the Truth"* (John 14:6).
    Let us *believe* Him.

II. He is *"the True Bread"* (John 6:32).
     Let us *feast* upon Him.

III. He is *"the True Vine"* (John 15:1).
      Let us *abide* in Him.

IV. He is *"the Holy and the True"* (Rev. 3:7).
     Let us be *holy* and *true* with Him.

V. He is *"the True Witness"* (Rev. 3:14).
    Let us *listen* to Him.

VI. He is *"the True Light"* (John 1:9).
     Let us be *illuminated* by Him.

VII. He is *"the True God"* (1 John 1:20).
      Let us *adore* Him.
      A. As "the Truth"—He delivers us from error.
      B. As "the True Bread"—He makes us independent of earth's joy.
      C. As "the True Vine"—He enables us to give joy to the Father who is seeking fruit.
      D. As "the True Witness"—He would restore our souls when we get into Laodicean lukewarmness.
      E. As "the Holy and the True"—He is the Pattern of what the church should be.
      F. As "the True Light"—The Pillar of Fire to guide us through the darkness of this world.
      G. As "the True God"—He is to receive equal honor with the Father, the Object of worship.

TWELVE BASKETS FULL

WHAT IS A CHRISTIAN?

What is a Christian? Many answers have been given to the above question. The servant girl's definition of Christians was very far out, who, when asked what Christians were, replied, "People who go to church and chapel, that talk about religion, and take the parson home to tea." That was her idea of a Christian, which, doubtless, she had gathered from the *professing* Christians with whom she had come in contact, but we need hardly say that this is not the Scriptural definition of a Christian.

> "Christian names are everywhere;
> Christian men are very rare."

The little girl was nearer the mark when she said, "A Christian is a born-again person"; for to be born again, is to be:

Saved by the grace of God. "By grace *are* ye saved through faith" (Eph. 2:8).

Sanctified in the Person of Christ. "Church of God . . . . to them that *are* sanctified in Christ Jesus" (1 Cor. 1:2).

Sealed with the Holy Spirit. "Grieve not the Holy Spirit of God, whereby ye *are* sealed unto the day of redemption" (Eph. 4:30).

Shining for the Lord Jesus. "Ye *are* the light of the world" (Matt. 5:14).

Serving with the Lord. "We *are* laborers together with God" (1 Cor. 3:9).

Slaves of the Lord. "Ye *are* not your own, for ye *are* bought with a price" (1 Cor. 6:19,20).

Surrendering to the Lord. "To whom ye yield yourselves servants to obey, his servants ye *are*" (Rom. 6:16). Note that in the Scriptures the word *"are"* occurs against each point, and, if they are carefully looked at, we shall find that a past definite act, a present fact, and a continuous consequence are referred to. What is a Christian? One has said, in defining a Christian, that he is:

"In faith, a *believer* in Christ.
In relationship, a *child* of God.
In character, a *saint*.
In influence, a *light*.
In communion, a *friend*.
In conflict, a *soldier*.
In experience, a *pilgrim*.
In expectation, an *heir*."

F. E. MARSH

THE LORD MY PORTION

I. My Savior (Matt. 1:21; 1 Tim. 1:15; Isa. 43:11).

II. My Substitute (Isa. 53:5; 2 Cor. 5:21; Rom. 5:8).

III. My Righteousness (Jer. 23:6; Rom. 10:4; Isa. 54:17).

IV. My Sanctification (1 Cor. 1; 2:30; Heb. 10:10).

V. My Example (Matt. 11:29; 1 Peter 2:21-23).

VI. My Teacher (Matt. 17:5; Isa. 50:4).

VII. My High Priest (Heb. 4:15; 7:26).

VIII. My Lord and Master (Matt. 23:10; John 13:13,14).

IX. My Brother (Rom. 8:29; Heb. 2:11,12).

X. My Friend (Prov. 18:24; S. of Sol. 5:16; John 15:14).

XI. My Keeper (Ps. 121:5; John 17:12; 1 Peter 1:5).

XII. My Wisdom (Prov. 3:13; 8:5; 1 Cor. 1:30).

XIII. My Shepherd (Ps. 23:1; Ezek. 34:23; John 10:11).

XIV. My Peace (Isa. 26:3; John 14:27; Eph. 2:14).

XV. My All in All (Col. 1:19; 2:10; 3:11).

TWELVE BASKETS FULL

PICTURE OF A RIGHTEOUS MAN

The Way of the Righteous (Ps. 1:6).
The Inheritance of the Righteous (Ps. 37:29).
The Gladness of the Righteous (Ps. 64:10).
The Flourishing of the Righteous (Ps. 92:12).
The Remembrance of the Righteous (Ps. 112:6).
The Thanksgiving of the Righteous (Ps. 140:13).
The Safety of the Righteous (Prov. 18:10).
The Recompense of the Righteous (Prov. 11:21).

PEGS FOR PREACHERS

CHRIST, THE SINCERE SHEPHERD

I am the good shepherd . . . (John 10:11).

These are the words of Jesus. He is our Good Shepherd. We are His sheep. See what He does as the Good Shepherd of our souls:

I. He Learns All About Us

"I know my sheep." "He calleth his own sheep by name." As the good Shepherd of our souls, the Lord Jesus Christ knows our names, our dispositions, our desires, our aims, our abilities, our faults, the degrees of consecration, and all that is to be known.

II. He Loves Us

"I lay down my life for the sheep." That tells the extent of the love of Christ for sinners. "Christ died for our sins according to the Scriptures." "God commendeth His love toward us, in that while we were yet sinners, Christ died for us." He loves us. His love is supreme and eternal.

III. He Leads Us

"Leadeth them out." "When he putteth forth his own sheep, he goeth before them." What a joy and satisfaction to follow such a Leader! We follow Him for we know His voice. He leads us by His presence, by His words, and by impression. He is the Good Shepherd, and His own should follow Him.

IV. He Longs for Us

"I am known of mine." He longs that we should know Him. "Learn of Me." As His sheep we "know his voice" and follow Him because we know He desires that we be near Him. He longs to protect His own from dangerous enemies, longs to lead His own to green pastures, and longs to feed His own with rich food from heaven.

V. He Lives for Us

"I am come that they might have life, and that they might have it more abundantly." "Because I live, ye shall live also." "I give unto them eternal life; and they shall never perish, neither shall any man pluck them out of my hand." He lives for us. In Him we may live forever.

SERMONS IN OUTLINE

MIRRORS OF CHRIST

But we all, with open face beholding as in a glass the glory
of the Lord, are changed into the same image from glory
to glory, even as by the Spirit of the Lord (2 Cor. 3:18).

The idea which Paul here announces is, that they who are much
in Christ's presence become mirrors of Him, reflecting more and
more permanently His image until they themselves perfectly
resemble Him. This assertion rests upon a well known law of our
nature. Our duty, then, if we would be transformed into the image
of Christ, is plain.

I. We Must Associate with Him; We Must Make Him Our
Most Constant Companion.
   A. We must not reflect Him in an occasional intermittent
way, but steadily and continually.
   B. We must live with Him.

II. We Must Be Careful to Turn Fully Round to Christ, So as
to Give a Full and Fair Reflection of Him. We must not
turn only half round, so as still to let other images fall on us.

III. We Must Stand in His Presence with Open Unveiled Face.
   A. We may wear a veil in the world, refusing to reflect it,
but when we return to the Lord we must uncover our face.
      1. A covered mirror reflects nothing.
      2. Perfect beauty may stand before it, but the napkin
shows no sign, offers no response.

IV. It Reduces Itself to This.
   A. Be much in the presence of Christ.
   B. Be so honestly enamored of Him that you will find Him
everywhere, and that your thoughts will fall back to Him as often as
your busy schedule permits.

V. Here Is Something We Can Do for Christ: We Can Reflect
Him.
   A. By reflecting Him we shall certainly extend the
knowledge of Him.
   B. Many who do not look at Him look at you.
      THREE HUNDRED OUTLINES ON THE NEW TESTAMENT

THE RESOURCES OF THE CHRISTIAN

For in Him dwelleth all the fullness of the Godhead bodily (Col. 2:9).

    I.   The Lord Jesus Christ Is Our Passover (1 Cor. 5:7).

    II.   The Lord Jesus Christ Is Our Salvation (Luke 2:27-30; 19:9; Isa. 12:2; 49:6).

    III.   The Lord Jesus Christ Is Our Life (Col. 3:4; 1 John 5:12).

    IV.   The Lord Jesus Christ Is Our Peace (Eph. 2:13,14; Col. 1:20).

    V.   The Lord Jesus Christ Is Our Wisdom, and Righteousness, and Sanctification, and Redemption (1 Cor. 1:30).

    VI.   The Lord Jesus Christ Is Our Strength (Phil. 3:13; Eph. 6:10; Ps. 18:2).

    VII.   The Lord Jesus Christ Is Our Victory (1 Cor. 15:57; Rom. 8:37).

TREASURES OF BIBLE TRUTH

LIFE IN CHRIST

Colossians 3:1-4

    I.   A Resurrected Life (v. 1a).

    II.   An Everlasting Life (vv. 1b,2).

    III.   A New Life (v. 3a).

    IV.   A Protected Life (v. 3b).

    V.   The Christ Life (v. 4a).

    VI.   A Hopeful Life (v. 4b).

    VII.   A Future Life (v. 4c).

SELECTED

HOW TO KNOW CHRIST BETTER

That I may know Him (Phil. 3:10).

To come to know Christ better was the first consuming desire of the heart of Paul after he met Him on the way to Damascus. We come to know Christ, first of all, by the new birth. Paul had passed this experience of grace. He applied himself definitely to know Christ better. All should long to know Him intimately. We make the following suggestions for reaching this goal:

I. Spend Much Time in Meditation.

After Paul met Christ his first move was to go alone with God for a long season of meditation on the meaning of the experience. During these months of meditation he received the Gospel "by the revelation of Jesus Christ" (Gal. 1:12).

The Lord gave Paul the clearest and most perfect understanding of the Gospel any man has had. We can come to know Christ better by quiet meditation.

II. Study Constantly the Lord's Message.

If we are to come to know Christ intimately, we must make the most of the Bible. The entire message of the Bible centers about Christ. We must know the Bible if we would know Christ well.

III. Speak Often with the Lord.

We come to know the people by talking with them and hearing them speak. So with the Lord Jesus we come to know Him by talking with Him. In prayer we speak to the Father and hear Him speak to us.

IV. Seek Fellowship with Other Christians.

Even though Paul did not go immediately to Jerusalem to see the apostles, he eventually did go, and had days of fellowship with Peter and James. Fellowship with consecrated and well-informed Christians may mean much to young Christians in coming to know Christ and His will and way for life.

V. Serve the Savior in Sincerity.

Jesus said, "Take My yoke upon you, and learn of Me." In other words, when a Christian gets under the problems of the Savior and serves with Him, he will come to know Him.

We will know Him when we think with Him. We will know Him when we suffer with Him. We will see His love for the lost and desire to have the same when we serve with Him. Paul served with Christ in a matchless way.

Set your heart to know Christ better and better. In meditation, Bible study, prayer, fellowship and service, seek to know Him and the fellowship of His suffering and the power of His resurrection.

SELECTED

THE CHRIST LIFE

For me to live is Christ, and to die is gain (Phil. 1:21).

   I.   A Life of Obedience (Acts 9:6; Heb. 10:9).

   II.   A Life of Service (1 Cor. 9:22).

   III.   A Life of Power (Matt. 28:18; Phil. 4:13).

   IV.   A Life of Sacrifice (John 15:13; Phil 3:7).

   V.   A Life of Separation (2 Cor. 6:14-18; Heb. 7:26).

   VI.   A Life of Suffering (2 Cor. 4:10,11).

   VII.   A Life of Victory (Phil. 2:9,10,11; 1 Cor. 15:57; Rom. 8:37).

TREASURES OF BIBLE TRUTH
WILLIAM H. SCHWEINFURTH

PAUL'S DESIRE IN PHILIPPIANS

To Know Christ (Phil. 3:10).

To Win Christ (Phil. 3:8).

To Be Conformed to Christ (Phil. 3:10).

To Magnify Christ (Phil. 1:20).

To Be Found in Christ (Phil. 3:9).

To Rejoice in Christ (Phil. 2:16).

To Be with Christ (Phil. 1:23).

PEGS FOR PREACHERS

CHRISTIAN CHARACTER

Be ye kind one to another, tenderhearted, forgiving one another,
even as God for Christ's sake hath forgiven you (Eph. 4:32).

This text gives the extent, the experience, the expression, and the best example of Christian character.

I. The Extent of Christian Character.

"Be ye kind." When a person is born again by the Spirit of God, he becomes a new creature in Christ. The inherent nature of this life will then become gentle, gracious, kind, good and benevolent. Such characteristics will dominate the entire life. These characteristics make up the real Christian personality.

II. The Experience in Christian Character.

"Be ye . . . tenderhearted." In its relations to others, the Christian character is easily moved to love, to pity, to sorrow, to sympathy. Such life will be able to place itself in the position of others and feel as they feel.

It will be moved with compassion for others as Jesus was moved.
It will quickly lend a helping hand to the person in need.
It will spend itself for others.

III. The Expression of Christian Character.

"Forgiving one another." Christian character will readily express itself toward others in being willing to forgive those who sin against it.

A forgiving spirit is Christlike, for on the Cross Christ prayed for those who crucified Him, saying, "Father, forgive them; for they know not what they do."

Jesus taught that His followers should be willing to forgive a limitless number of times. Christian character expresses itself in willingness to forgive.

IV. The Example of Christian Character.

"Even as God for Christ's sake hath forgiven you." The example of God the Father is here held up as the ideal for the Christian. This is the most sublime ideal. This is the highest example of Christian character. It is the highest and holiest ideal and should be before every Christian.

SELECTED

OUR WONDERFUL SAVIOR

. . . His name shall be called Wonderful . . . (Isa. 9:6).

W—Wonderful in His Work (John 7:21; 9:4; 17:4).

O—Wonderful in His Offering (Heb. 10:10, 14, 18).

N—Wonderful in His Nature (Col. 2:9; John 10:30; 14:9).

D—Wonderful in His Deeds (John 5:19; Mark 7:37).

E—Wonderful in His Example (1 Peter 2:21).

R—Wonderful in His Redemption (Col. 1:14; Eph. 1:7; 1 Peter 1:18-20).

F—Wonderful in His Forbearance (Mark 15:3-5).

U—Wonderful in His Union (John 17:21,22,23).

L—Wonderful in His Love (John 15:13; 13:1).

TREASURES OF BIBLE TRUTH

WHAT CHRISTIANS SHALL BE

Eye hath not seen, nor ear heard . . . the things which God hath prepared for them that love Him (1 Cor. 2:9).

   I.   They Shall Be Changed (1 Cor. 15:51,52).

   II.   They Shall Be Caught Up (1 Thess. 4:17).

  III.   They Shall Be Like Christ (1 John 3:2).

  IV.   They Shall Appear with Christ (Col. 3:4).

   V.   They Shall Be Judges (1 Cor. 6:2,3).

  VI.   They Shall Be Priests (Rev. 20:6; 1:6; 5:10).

VII.   They Shall Be with Christ Forever (1 Thess. 4:17,18).

TREASURES OF BIBLE TRUTH
WILLIAM H. SCHWEINFURTH

STEPS IN TRUE CONSECRATION

2 Chronicles 17

The right attitude of the soul to the Lord is the secret of true consecration.

I. **Companioning with the Lord (v. 3).** The Lord was with Jehoshaphat, because he was with the Lord by obedience to His Word. To be is to have.

II. **Directing to the Lord (v. 4).** As the ship will be kept on its right course as the helmsman is guided by the compass, so the believer will be right in life as he directs his way by the written Word of the living God.

III. **Blessing from the Lord (v. 5).** The way of Jehoshaphat was established, because he was steadfast, for the time being in the way of the Lord. If we are faithful to the Lord by obeying His Word, He will be faithful to us in giving us His blessing.

IV. **Encouraged in the Lord (v. 6).** The king was encouraged (margin) in the ways of the Lord by the Lord's blessing. There is no fear of the Lord's blessing; the only fear is, lest we should fail to fear the Lord who blesses.

V. **Word of the Lord (v. 9).** To teach the Word of the Lord is to impart the greatest blessing upon mankind. See Psalm 19:7-11 as to what the Word of God is and does.

VI. **Power through the Lord (v. 10).** The greatest influence that any man can exert is the influence that comes from the presence of God with him.

VII. **Offering unto the Lord (v. 16).** To give ourselves to the Lord, and to allow ourselves to remain in His hands, is the very essence of consecration (Rom. 6:13; 12:1).

F. E. MARSH

DELIVERANCE

*For we that are in this tabernacle do groan,
being burdened . . . (2 Cor. 5:4).*

I. **The Christian's Present Condition**
    A. The body is a tent—*Movable.*
    B. It is earthly in its elements—*Tendencies.*
    C. It is mortal—*There are rents in it already.*
    D. The soul is a *sojourner* in it.

II. **His Circumstances—"Burdened"**
    A. By the vicissitudes of life.
    B. By persecutions.
    C. By temptations.
    D. By the remains of sin.

III. **His Desire—"Groan"**
    A. For deliverance.
    B. For a permanent house—*Home.*

PULPIT GERMS

DAILY THINGS

I. Daily Bread. Do you feed on it? (Matt. 6:11)

II. Daily Cross. Do you carry it? (Luke 9:23)

III. Daily Preaching. Do you do it? (Acts 5:42)

IV. Daily Searching. Do you enjoy it? (Acts 17:11)

V. Daily Dying. Do you believe it? (1 Cor. 15:31)

VI. Daily Exhorting. Do you love it? (Heb. 3:13)

VII. Daily Watching. Do you practice it? (Prov. 8:34)

INGLIS

THE OLD AND THE NEW

*Old things have passed away, behold all things
are become new (2 Cor. 5:17).*

I. The Old
   A. Spiritual darkness; blind in sin (Eph. 4:18).
   B. Satan's bondservants (Prov. 5:22; 2 Tim. 2:26).
   C. Children of the devil (John 8:44).
   D. Morally defiled (Isa. 1:6; Mark 7:21,22).
   E. An evil conscience.
   F. An unholy life. "Such were some of you" (1 Cor. 6:9,10).
   G. Pleasure in sin.
   H. Without hope and without God in the world (Eph. 2:12).

II. The New
   A. Eyes opened; heart enlightened (John 8:12; 1 John 1:6).
   B. Free from the bondage of sin (Gal. 5:1).
   C. Children of God (1 John 3:1,2).
   D. Morally pure; affections sanctified (Matt. 5:8).
   E. A good conscience (Acts 24:16; 1 John 3:21).
   F. A holy life.
   G. Pleasure in doing good. Joy in the service of Christ.
   H. A lively hope of a blessed immortality (1 Peter 1:3,4).

100 SERMON OUTLINES

POWER OF THE SPIRIT

I. Power Promised. "Ye shall receive power" (Acts 1:8).

II. Power Sought. "Continued . . . in prayer" (Acts 1:14).

III. Power Given. "All filled with the Holy Ghost" (Acts 2:4).

IV. Power in Action. "They were pricked in their heart" (Acts 2:37).

INGLIS

THE DUTY OF DISCIPLES

Seek ye first the kingdom of God, and
His righteousness (Matt. 6:33).

It should be the supreme purpose of everyone to seek the kingdom of God. We study the text through five questions.

I.   What Is to Be Done?

"Seek." Put your heart into this enterprise. Seek earnestly, diligently, enthusiastically, steadily, with your whole life, hands, head and heart.

II.   Who Is to Seek?

"Ye." All who believe in the Lord Jesus Christ. All who name the Name of Christ. All who are members of His Church and all who have a desire to do His way and will. All who have had an experience of grace and possess a new heart, a new purpose, a new hope, a new outlook, and a new Master. "Seek ye."

III.   When Shall We Seek?

"First." In time. In aim. In activity.

IV.   What Shall We Seek?

His kingdom, and His righteousness. Seek to be right in every relation of life, in relation to God, to Christ, to the Church, to all Christians, to all sinners.

V.   Why Should We Seek?

Because when we attain righteousness and seek the kingdom, all lesser blessings will be added unto us. When we seek the kingdom and righteousness of the Lord, He will see that we have all necessary food and clothing and raiment. It is a promise of the Lord.

SERMONS IN OUTLINE

WITH WINGS AS EAGLES

They that wait upon the Lord shall renew their strength;
they shall mount up with wings as eagles (Isa. 40:31).

Many metaphors and similes are used in Scripture to help the people of God to understand themselves: sheep, salt, light, branches, soldiers, leaven, etc.

In the text the man of God is compared to the greatest of the fowls of the air, the eagle.

I. The Eagle Is Noted for Great Strength.
    A. Christians should be "strong in the Lord," etc.
    B. Christians should never be "weary in well-doing."

II. The Eagle Is Noted for Its Farsightedness.
    A. "The Christian on his knees sees more than the philosopher on tiptoes."
    B. Stephen's "eagle eyes" —vision of the Son of God.
    C. Daniel's window open toward Jerusalem.

III. The Eagle Rises Above the World, Which Is Enveloped by Gases, Smoke, Dust and Clouds.
    A. The Christian rises above the sordid things of the world.
    B. The Christian walks on the earth, but his head is above the clouds.
    C. Man's soul longs for freedom from sin.

IV. The Eagle Is Noted for Longevity.
    A. The Christian will live forever.

SNAPPY SERMON STARTERS
PAUL E. HOLDCRAFT

THE KEEPER AND THE KEPT

Isaiah 26:3

The Divine Keeper—"Thou wilt keep"
The Gracious Keeper—"In perfect peace"
The Kept Described—"Whose mind is stayed on Thee"
The Means Disclosed—"He trusteth in Thee"

JOHN RITCHIE

THE AIM AND ATTITUDE OF FAITH

Joshua 6:8-20

I. The *place* of faith. "Before the Lord" (Josh. 6:8; Phil. 2:12).

II. The *testimony* of faith. "Blowing with the trumpets" (v. 9; 1 Thess. 1:8).

III. The *attitude* of faith. "Until I bid you" (v. 10; Col. 2:6).

IV. The *rest* of faith. "Lodged in the camp" (v. 11; 1 John 2:28).

V. The *activity* of faith. "Rose early . . . took up" (v. 12; James 2:22-26).

VI. The *continuance* of faith. "Went on continually" (vv. 13,14; John 8:31).

VII. The *perfection* of faith. "Seven times" (v. 15; 1 Thess. 3:10).

VIII. The *boldness* of faith. "Shout" (v. 16; Acts 4:13).

IX. The *assurance* of faith. "The Lord hath given" (v. 16; 1 John 5:10,11).

X. The *recognition* of faith. "Devoted (margin) to the Lord" (v. 17; 1 Peter 3:5).

XI. The *separation* of faith. "Keep yourselves from the accursed thing" (v. 18; 2 Cor. 7:1).

XII. The *service* of faith. To bring the consecrated things "into the treasury of the Lord" (v. 19; 1 Cor. 6:20).

XIII. The *triumph* of faith. "The wall fell down flat" (v. 20; 1 John 5:4,5).

XIV. The *possession* of faith. "They took the city" (v. 20; Gen. 22:17).

Thus, in these verses, we have in miniature what faith *is*, what faith *brings*, and what faith *does*.

F. E. MARSH

A LIFE OF FAITH

. . . as it is written, The just shall live by faith (Rom. 1:17).

Faith is essential to all life. Without faith it is impossible to please God. This text shows that faith is the source, the support, and the success of life.

I.   Faith Is the Source of Life

"By faith." Only by faith in the Lord Jesus Christ can one attain unto eternal life. It is believe and live. "Believe on the Lord Jesus Christ, and thou shalt be saved." "He that believeth on the Son hath eternal life." Eternal life is possible only by grace through faith in the Lord Jesus Christ. Real life begins with faith in Christ.

II.   Faith Is the Support of Life

"Shall live by faith." Faith in the Lord and in His power to help is the support of life. "Who is he that overcometh the world, but he that believeth that Jesus is the Son of God." Faith is the force that *supports* life and *sustains* life unto the end. Faith *enriches* life. Faith *enlarges* life. Faith *enables* life. Faith *increases* life.

III.   Faith Is the Success of Life

"The righteous shall live by faith." Faith is the force that leads on to righteousness. It is the power that will appropriate the righteousness of Christ for the life of the individual in the world. Believe in Christ, appropriate His grace, and follow Him is the only way to succeed in the Christian life.

By faith live and serve. "Without faith it is impossible to please God."

SERMONS IN OUTLINE
JEROME O. WILLIAMS

THREE DESIRES OF THE SAINT IN PSALM 119

"Make me to know the way" (v. 27)—Understanding
"Make me to go in the path" (v. 36)—Obedience
"Make Thy face to shine upon" (v. 135)—Communion
JOHN RITCHIE

GREAT FAITH

O woman, great is thy faith; be it unto thee even
as thou wilt (Matt. 15:28).

"Faith is the substance of things hoped for, the evidence of things not seen."

I. **"Great Faith" Leads to Great Undertakings**
It was a great undertaking for this woman to come to Christ.

II. **"Great Faith" Brings about Great Expectations**
She expected the Savior to heal her daughter. We often expect no great results from our labors, because we have not this great faith.

III. **"Great Faith" Awakens Great Earnestness**
She cried, and fell at His feet and worshiped Him. Look at the earnestness of Knox, Luther, Wesley, etc. They all had great faith.

IV. **"Great Faith" Conquers Great Difficulties**
First it is said, "He answered her not a word." But she kept on. Next He said He was not sent but to the lost sheep of the house of Israel. Still she is not discouraged. Next He said, "It was not meet to take the children's bread and cast it to the dogs." She answered, "Truth, O Lord," etc. What difficulties have not been overcome by men of undaunted courage and faith!

V. **"Great Faith" Achieves Great Victories**
"Be it unto thee even as thou wilt" and her daughter was made whole (Mark 9:23; Matt. 17:20; Heb. 11:30-40).

100 SERMON OUTLINES

Dwight L. Moody described three kinds of faith in Jesus Christ: struggling faith, which is like a man in deep water; clinging faith, which is like a man hanging to the side of a boat; and resting faith, which finds a man safely within the boat, and able moreover to reach out with a hand to help someone else.

THE ANTIDOTE TO FEAR

Fear thou not; for I am with thee . . . (Isa. 41:10).

Fear is common to man, increased by, if it does not originate in a consciousness of sin. The text indicates three reasons why the Christian should not be afraid.

I. God's Presence

"I am *with* thee"

Powerful, wise, loving.

II. God's Relationship

"I am *thy* God"

These words imply on our part reverence, obedience and submission; on His part guardianship and blessing. We naturally take special care of that which is our own.

III. God's Promise

A. "I will *strengthen* thee"—fortify your heart against trial and suffering.

B. "I will *help* thee"—render you personal assistance; direct, protect, fight with and for you.

C. "I will uphold thee"

"The right hand of My righteousness." My faithful right hand: i.e., a hand that could be relied upon.

The right hand is generally used for work.

The right hand is offered in friendship.

The right hand is placed on those whom we wish to honor.

THE PREACHER'S TREASURY

Faith is more like a verb than a noun . . . Faith *accepts* the Word of God, *affirms* confidence in that Word and *acts* upon it. You never really get going until you act upon what you accept and affirm. Then you are "faithing" your way along.

VANCE HAVNER, *PEACE IN THE VALLEY*

FIVE SMOOTH STONES FROM THE BROOK

The way to slay the Goliaths of sin and unbelief is simply to take the Word of God and hurl it at them. In these days of light regard for God's testimony, when even many clergy are seeking to destroy faith in the plenary inspiration of the Scriptures, it behoves us to stand like heroes in defense of "the faith once for all delivered to the saints." Goliath of old defiantly sneered at the youth who came out to do battle with him, but God was with David, and soon demonstrated to the waiting expectant hosts that He could use the "weak things of this world" to accomplish His divine purposes. He inspired David to take "five smooth stones from the brook." These, with the shepherd's sling, constituted David's entire armament; but with these he slew the giant, and Israel's host reaped a mighty victory, while God got the glory. So, if the servant of God will only heed His instruction, and seek to become thoroughly furnished by diligent study of His Word, rightly dividing the same, he will "become mighty to the pulling down of strongholds."

There are five fundamental facts in the Bible, arranged in very beautiful order by the Holy Spirit, namely: *Man's Ruin, Man's Redemption, Man's Regeneration, Man's Sanctification,* and *Man's Glorification.* They are Five Smooth Stones from the Brook of God.

I. Man's Ruin.

"If one died for all, then were all dead" (2 Cor. 5:14; see also Eph. 2:1-3; Gen. 6:5; Isa. 1:4-6).

II. Man's Redemption.

"For as much as ye know that ye were not redeemed with corruptible things. . . . but with the precious blood of Christ, as of a lamb without blemish and without spot" (1 Peter 1:18,19). See also Leviticus 17:11; Exodus 12:14; and for many other passages on this theme trace out the references.

III. Man's Regeneration.

"Verily, verily, I say unto thee, except a man be born again, he cannot see the kingdom of God" (John 3:3). Also 1 Peter 1:23; James 1:18; John 1:13; 10:28; 1 Cor. 3:6,7.

IV. Man's Sanctification.

"I beseech you therefore, brethren, by the mercies of God," etc. (Rom. 12:1,2).

A. The God, or judicial, side of the question (1 Cor. 1:30; Col. 3:3; 2:10; Heb. 5:9).

B. The man, or experimental, side of the question (1 Cor. 6:15,16; 1 John 2:15-17; Col. 3:1,2).

V. Man's Glorification.

"Beloved, now are we the sons of God; and it doth not yet appear what we shall be; but we know that when He shall appear, we shall be like Him; for we shall see Him as He is" (1 John 3:2; John 14:1-3).

J. E. WOLF

WHAT GOD IS TO HIS PEOPLE

A. Almighty God, to bless us. "I am the *Almighty God*" (Gen. 17:1).

B. Blessed God, to cheer us. "Glorious gospel of the *blessed God*" (1 Tim. 1:11).

C. Compassionate God, to bear with us. "For the Lord's portion is His people," etc. (Deut. 32:9-13).

D. Defending God, to protect us. "The Lord is my Strength," etc. (Ex. 15:2,3).

E. Eternal God, to secure us. "The *eternal God* is thy Refuge" (Deut. 33:27).

F. Faithful God, to assure us. "Judged him *faithful* Who had promised" (Heb. 11:11).

G. Gracious God, to bless us. "Thou art a *gracious God*, and merciful, slow to anger," etc. (Jonah 4:2).

H. Holy God, to sanctify us. "I am God . . . the *Holy One*" (Hosea 11:9).

I. Indwelling God, to establish us. "God is *in the midst* of her; she shall *not be moved*" (Ps. 46:5).

J. Just God, to clear us. "A *just God* and a *Savior*" (Isa. 45:21).

K. Kind God, to supply us. "Who crowneth thee with *lovingkindness*" (Ps. 103:4).

L. Loving God, to cherish us. "Yea, I have *loved thee*" (Jer. 31:3).

M. Mighty God, to deliver us. "With His *mighty power*" (Deut. 4:37).

N. Near God, to sustain us. "He is *near* that justifieth me" (Isa. 50:8).

O. Omniscient God, to watch over us. "Behold He that *keepeth* Israel," etc. (Ps. 121:4-7).

P. Powerful God, to strengthen us. "The Lord stood with me and *strengthened* me" (2 Tim. 4:17).

Q. Quickening God, to change us. "Hath *quickened* us together with Christ" (Eph. 2:5).

R. Righteous God, to justify us. "Establish the *just*: for the *righteous God* trieth the hearts and reins" (Ps. 7:9).

S. Saving God, to free us. "This is our God . . . . and He will *save* us" (Isa. 25:9).

T. Truth-keeping God, to encourage us. "Which keepeth *truth* forever" (Ps. 146:6).

U. Unchanging God, to secure us. "I am the Lord, I *change not*" (Mal. 3:6).

V. Victorious God, to overcome for us. "Thanks be to God, which giveth us the *victory*" (1 Cor. 15:57).

W. Wise God, to enlighten us. "If any lack *wisdom*, let him *ask* of God," etc. (James 1:5).

Y. Yearning God, to look after us. "Yet will I not *forget* thee. Behold I have *graven* thee upon the palms of My hands" (Isa. 49:15,16).

Z. Zealous God, to keep us. "According to His Divine power hath given unto us all things," etc. (2 Peter 1:3).

F. E. MARSH

GOD'S PEOPLE

But ye are a peculiar people (1 Peter 2:9).

   I. God's People Are a *Professing* People.

  II. God's People Are a *Separated* People.

 III. God's People Are a *Suffering* People.

 IV. God's People Are a *Praying* People.

  V. God's People Are a *Sanctified* People.

 VI. God's People Are a *Blessed* People.

PULPIT GERMS

GODLY LIVING

Having your conversation honest among the Gentiles; that whereas they speak against you as evil-doers, they may by your good works, which they behold, glorify God in the day of visitation (1 Peter 2:12).

  I. The World's Treatment of Christians
- A. Enmity
- B. Defamation
- C. Perversion of the truth
- D. Aggravation of circumstances

 II. The Behavior Recommended
- A. Honesty
- B. Consistency
- C. Truthfulness
- D. Purity
- E. Fidelity
- F. Circumspection

III. The Results That Will Obtain
- A. God will be glorified.
- B. His religion will be honored.
- C. Men will be saved.

PULPIT GERMS

PROGRESS IN GRACE

I. Saved by Grace (Eph. 2:8).
    A. We need to acquaint ourselves with the grace of God: that wonderful new thing that Christ revealed to men.
        1. He showed it long ago in His life, teaching, and death for sinners, but many still do not know anything about it: know no other way of holiness but by works of law.
    B. We need to verify in our own experience that a saving virtue resides in the grace of God.
        1. Let us try to realize what it means that the God we had offended by our sin, whom we had ignored by our indifference has ever been looking on us in love and planning to make us fit to enjoy Himself forever. Has the grace of God saved you from sin?

II. Standing in Grace: established in it (Rom. 5:2).

III. Taught by Grace (Titus 2:12).
    A. We cannot possibly be affected by the grace of God without its having a revolutionary effect on our conduct.

IV. Growing in Grace (2 Peter 3:18).
    A. As the years go on we get larger and fuller views of God's grace.

V. Speaking in Grace (Col. 4:6).
    A. We shall not be able to keep the blessing to ourselves; we shall speak of the grace of God and in the grace of God.
    B. Our way of speaking to others should give them some idea of how Christ spoke to men.
    C. Our conversation is to be always with grace, tempered with salt which saves from corruption.

VI. Ministering Grace (Eph. 4:29).
    A. Our relationship with others should be of such a character that it helps to form them also in the likeness of Christ.
    B. All our conduct toward others should tend to show them more and more of the beauty of the grace as revealed in Christ.

VII. Who Is Sufficient for These Things?
    We can neither receive nor show the grace of God in our own strength, but only through Christ's enabling, in answer to prayer.

100 SERMON OUTLINES

THE PROOF OF GOD'S LOVE

But God commendeth His love toward us, in that, while
we were yet sinners, Christ died for us (Rom. 5:8).

In broad and striking contrast with the comparative poverty of our human love, Paul sets the greatness and the wonder of God's love to man.

I.   God Does Not Ask Us to Take His Love Simply on Trust.

A.   To doubt His love would be an affront to the reason as well as a discredit to the heart.

B.   Our faith is not vain in the sense of being unsupported by proofs.

II.   What Is the Proof?

A.   Christ died for us.

1.   The death of Christ was the manifestation of the infinite love of God to man, and was designed to prove it to the world. It was not necessary for Christ to die to make God love us, but Christ died to show that God already loved us.

B.   While we were yet sinners He died for us.

1.   If He had died for good men it would have been an amazing act of love; but it was more.

2.   A profound sense of sin is always associated with a profound realization of the greatness of the love of God.

III.   The Cross of Christ Is a Present Reality.

A.   The Apostle does not say God has proved His love toward us, as if it were something away in the past; but he says it is a proof going on still.

1.   The Cross speaks to the heart of man with the same tenderness and power as it did to the eye-witnesses of the love and sorrow of His passion and death.

THREE HUNDRED OUTLINES ON THE NEW TESTAMENT

THE GOOD SHEPHERD

I am the Good Shepherd (John 10:11)

When our Lord calls Himself the Good Shepherd, is He using a title which has lost its value since He has ceased to live visibly upon the earth? This title has a true meaning for Christians, and an attractive power which is all its own. To enter into the full force of this image, we must know something really of ourselves, and something really of our Savior.

I. **As the Good Shepherd, He Knows His Sheep.**

He knows us individually, not merely as we seem to be, but as we are. It is because He thus knows us that He is able to help, guide and feed us.

II. **He Has a Perfect Sympathy with Each One of Us.**

He is not a hard guardian, without any sort of feeling for our individual difficulties, yet this sympathy is guided by perfect prudence. The Good Shepherd has proportioned our duties, our trials, our advantages, our reverses, to our real needs, capacities and characters.

III. **He Is Unselfish Above All, as the Good Shepherd.**

He seeks not *ours*, but *us*. He gains nothing by watching, guiding, feeding such as us. He gave His life for the sheep. He gave it once for all nearly twenty centuries ago; but His death is just as powerful to deliver us from the onset of the wolf as then. Self-sacrifice such as that on Calvary does not lose its virtue by the lapse of years.

THREE HUNDRED OUTLINES ON THE NEW TESTAMENT

WHAT CHRIST GIVES HIS PEOPLE
AS RECORDED IN JOHN'S GOSPEL

His *Life* for their Redemption (10:11)
His *Flesh* for their Sustenance (6:51)
His *Peace* for their Enjoyment (14:27)
His *Example* for their Pattern (13:16)
His *Word* for their Sanctification (17:8, 17)
His *Glory* for their Home (17:22)

JOHN RITCHIE

GRACE

By grace we are *called* (1 Tim. 1:9; Gal. 1:15).
By grace we are *forgiven* (Eph. 1:7).
By grace we are *saved* (Eph. 2:5, 8).
By grace we are *justified* (Rom. 3:24; Titus 3:7).
By grace we are made *possessors of eternal life* (Rom. 5:15).
By grace we are made *righteous* (Rom. 5:19).
By grace we are *strengthened* (2 Tim. 2:1).
We are to *stand* in grace (1 Peter 5:12; Rom. 5:2).
We are to *grow* in grace (2 Peter 3:18).
We are to be *established* in grace (Heb. 13:9).
We are to *testify* of the gospel of grace (Acts 20:24).
We are to look to the word of grace for *power* (Acts 20:32).
Grace changes our *position* (Rom. 6:14).
Grace changes our *life* (1 Tim. 1:13,14; 1 Cor. 15:10).
Grace changes our *conversation* (2 Cor. 1:12).
Grace changes our *thoughts* (Rom. 12:3).
Grace gives us *strength* to meet every trial (2 Cor. 12:7-9).
Wisdom for Christian work (1 Cor. 3:9,10).
To the *least* child of God it is given (Eph. 3:8; Eph. 4:7).
A *sufficient* supply for all time. "Enough for *each*, enough for *all*,
    enough for *evermore*" (2 Cor. 9:8).
No danger of it running short (James 4:6; 1 Peter 1:2).
We have a "God of all grace"—and a Savior "full of grace" to draw
    from (1 Peter 5:10; John 1:14).
Our whole salvation is of grace (Titus 2:11).
It was grace that brought Christ from the glory down to earth (2 Cor.
    8:9; Phil. 2:6-8).
It is grace that takes us from earth into the glory (Eph. 2:6; Eph. 1:20,21).

Oh! the fullness of His grace,
Rich and boundless, great and free;
Making sinners, poor and lost,
Heirs of God, with Him to be:
Human lips would fail to tell
Half the sweet and wondrous
    story;

How He brings us by His grace.
All the way from *sin* to *glory*;
But when we reach that glory bright,
    and our faith is changed to sight,
Then these tongues shall sweetly sing
    all the praises of our King.

SELECTED

GROWTH IN GRACE

Grow in grace (2 Peter 3:18).

I. False Marks of Growth in Grace
  A. Increasing religious knowledge.
  B. Pleasure in conversing on religious topics.
  C. Pleasure in hearing the Word.
  D. Zeal for the cause of religion.

II. The True Marks of Growth in Grace
  A. An increasing humility.
  B. A self-denying spirit.
  C. Simplicity and sincerity of mind.
  D. Increasing hatred of falsehood and artifice.

III. The Means to Be Used
  A. Secret prayer.
  B. A diligent perusal of the Word.
  C. Careful self-examination.

THE PULPIT SYNOPSIS
RICHARD COPE

THREEFOLD LOVE OF GOD

1 John 3:1

I. Manner—"Behold, what manner"

II. Meaning—"Called the sons of God"

III. Measure—"World knoweth us not"

1,000 SERMON OUTLINES
T. W. CALLAWAY
J. ELLIS

THE CHILD OF GOD SHOULD BE STEADFAST

In Faith (1 Peter 5:9).
In Work (1 Cor. 15:58).
In Looking (Acts 1:10).
In Doctrine (Acts 2:42).
In Mind (Ruth 1:18).   PEGS FOR PREACHERS

WHAT A CHILD OF GOD SHOULD HAVE

Christ in his heart (Col. 1:27)
Glory in his face (Acts 6:15)
The Spirit as his teacher (John 14:26)
Fear of God to guide him (Prov. 8:13)
Path of holiness to walk in (Isa. 35:11)
Heaven as his destination (John 14:2)   PEGS FOR PREACHERS

HOLY SPIRIT AND HIS WORK

The Spirit of the living God (2 Cor. 3:3).

God deals with men through His Holy Spirit in this age.

I.   How He Works FOR Man.
  A.   By Applying the Word (Acts 28:28; 1 Tim. 3:16).
  B.   By promulgating the Word (Acts 2:4; Acts 13:2).
  C.   By interpreting the Word (John 16:13; Acts 8:39).

II. How He Works IN Man.
  A.   In conviction (John 16:8).
  B.   In enlightenment (John 14:26).
  C.   In regeneration (John 3:5).

III. How He Works BY Man.
  A.   Man is prepared for work (Elisha for Israel).
  B.   Work is prepared for man (Nineveh for Jonah).
  C.   Work is revealed to man (Exodus to Moses).

IV. How He Works WITH Man.
  A.   His comforting presence (John 16:7).
  B.   His powerful assistance (John 14:12).
  C.   His sanctifying indwelling (Rom. 15:16).

TOOLS FOR THE MASTER'S WORK

TRUTHS CONNECTED WITH THE HOLY SPIRIT

I. The Holy Spirit
   A. Convicts the World (John 16:8-12).
   B. Regenerates the Believing one (John 3:5-7; 1 John 5:7).
   C. Indwells the Child of God (John 14:17).
   D. Seals the Saint (Eph. 1:13).
   E. Is the Comforter and Guide (John 15:26; 16:13).
   F. Is the Promise of the Holy Anointing (1 John 2:20).
   G. Is the Earnest of Coming Glory (Eph. 1:14).

II. The Christian Is Exhorted to
   A. Be Filled with the Spirit (Eph. 5:18).
   B. Pray in the Spirit (Jude 20; Eph. 6:18).
   C. Sing in the Spirit (Eph. 5:19).
   D. Worship in the Spirit (John 4:23; Phil. 3:3).
   E. Walk in the Spirit (Gal. 5:16).
   F. Be Led by the Spirit (Gal. 5:18).
   G. Remember His Body is the Temple of the Holy Spirit
(1 Cor. 6:19).   TWELVE BASKETS FULL

REDEMPTION

The word means "to buy back" and set free. There is a Redemption by Blood and by Power.

Man's Ruin (Isa. 52:3; John 8:34; Rom. 6:20)

Man's Helplessness (Ps. 49:7; Micah 6:7)

A Redeemer Povided (Job 33:24; Ps. 111:9)

Redemption by Blood (Eph. 1:7; Acts 20:28; Heb. 9:12)

Redemption by Power (Eph. 1:13-44; 4:30; Rom. 8:23)

Redemption from Iniquity (Titus 2:14; 1 Peter 1:18)

Redemption from the Curse (Gal. 3:13; Ps. 103:4)

Redemption of Body (Rom. 8:23; Phil. 3:20 R.V.)
                     500 BIBLE SUBJECTS

THE TOUCH OF JESUS:
Its Power Physically and Spiritually

Gives Life (Mark 5:41; John 11:25,26; Eph. 2:5)

Cleanses the Foulest (Matt. 8:3; 1 Cor. 6:11; Eph. 5:27)

Heals the Fever-Stricken (Matt. 8:15; John 14:27; Heb. 4:3)

Opens Blind Eyes (Matt. 9:29; Mark 8:22-25; John 8:12)

Makes Dumb Lips Speak (Mark 7:32-35; Isa. 35:6; Acts 2:4; 19:6)

Cleanses Long-Standing Secret Disease (Matt. 9:20; Ps. 19:12; Ex. 15:26)

Heals Perfectly (Matt. 14:36; Acts 3:16)

Heals Wounds Caused by Disciples (Luke 22:51; 23:34)

Banishes Fear (Matt. 27:7; John 14:1; Heb. 13:6)

Stays Sorrow (Luke 7:13-14; Ps. 58:12; John 14:27)

Welcomes Little Ones (Mark 10:13-16; Matt. 18:2-5).

Meets Every Need (Luke 6:19; 2 Cor. 7:9)

SERMONS IN A NUTSHELL

REST

There are at least three words translated "rest" in the New Testament.

I.   *Anapausis* - "an *up* rest," as in Matthew 11:28

II. *Katapausis* - "A *down* rest," as in Hebrews 4:4

III. *Sabbatismos* - "a *Sabbath* rest," as in Hebrews 4:9

IV. Kinds of Rest
  A. Rest for the Sinner (Matt. 11:28)—At the Cross
  B. Rest for the Saint (Matt. 11:29)—In Subjection
  C. Rest in the Lord (Ps. 36:7)—In Confidence
  D. Rest with the Lord (2 Thess. 1:7)—In Glory
  E. Rest that Remains (Heb. 4:9)—Eternal

500 BIBLE SUBJECTS

THE FRUIT OF THE SPIRIT

But the fruit of the Spirit is love, joy, peace, long-suffering, gentleness, goodness, faith, meekness, temperance (Gal. 5:22,23).

We have "the works of the flesh," but we do not read of "the fruits of the Spirit," but in the singular number—fruit.

The nine graces are one fruit.

I. **All the Other Fruits of the Spirit Are Only the Expansion of the First.**
    A. Joy is love *triumphing*.
    B. Peace is love *resting*.
    C. Long-suffering is love under the *great trials*.
    D. Gentleness is love under the *little trials* of life.
    E. Goodness is love going forth into *action*.
    F. Faith is love sitting and *receiving* back again to its own bosom.
    G. Meekness is love *controlling* the passions of the mind.
    H. Temperance, the same love *subduing* the passions of the body.

    The law of the Spirit is all contained in one word, and the unity of the whole Christian character is "love." Fruit is not fruit if it is not sweet. What is anything to God until there is love in it? Therefore, love stands first.

II. **There Is a Law of Growth About the Spirit of God in a Man.**
    A. This is as sure as the law which regulates the growth and development of any plant.
        1. This truth is wrapped up in the metaphor "the fruit of the Spirit."
        2. If there is not advance in the image of Christ, it is because the work of the Holy Ghost is obstructed, for the Spirit, in Himself, always essentially grows.

III. **To Be Fruit-Bearers We Must Be Engrafted into the True Vine.**
    A. If there is one state more solemn than another it is the leafy state.
        1. What if Jesus, drawing nigh to any one of us and finding nothing but leaves, should punish the barrenness which is willful by the barrenness which is judicial: "No man eat fruit of thee hereafter forever"?

THREE HUNDRED OUTLINES ON THE NEW TESTAMENT

THE HOLY SPIRIT

I. **What He Is**
- A. He is a *Person*. "Descended in bodily shape" (Luke 3:22).
- B. He always *Existed*. "The eternal Spirit" (Heb. 9:14).
- C. He is *Omniscient*. "Searcheth all things" (1 Cor. 2:10).
- D. He is *Omnipresent*. "Whither shall I go," etc. (Ps. 139:7-11).
- E. He is *Omnipotent*. Raised the dead witnesses (Rev. 11:11).

II. **His Operations**
- A. *Convinces*. "Convince the world of sin" (John 16:8).
- B. *Quickens*. "Quicken . . . by His Spirit" (Rom. 8:11).
- C. *Indwells*. "If the Spirit . . . dwell in you" (Rom. 8:9).
- D. *Comforts*. "Another Comforter" (John 14:16-17).
- E. *Seals*. "Sealed with that Holy Spirit" (Eph. 1:13).
- F. *Reveals*. "Revealed . . by the Spirit" (Eph. 3:5).
- G. *Sanctifies*. "Sanctified . . . by the Spirit" (1 Cor. 6:11).
- H. *Leads*. "Led by the Spirit of God" (Rom. 8:14).
- I. *Witnesses*. "The Spirit itself beareth witness" (Rom. 8:16).

BIBLE THEMES FOR BUSY WORKERS

HEAVEN: THE ETERNAL CITY

Glorious things are spoken of thee, O city of God (Ps. 87:3).

I. **A Place of Supreme Happiness.**
"Fullness of Joy" (Ps. 16:11).
"God shall wipe away all tears" (Rev. 7:17).

II. **A Place of Surpassing Beauty.**
"Eye hath not seen nor ear heard" (1 Cor. 2:9).
"The half was not told" (1 Kings 10:7)

III. **A Place of Revelation.**
"Now we know in part, then . . ." (1 Cor. 13:12).

IV. **A Place of Freedom from Pain.**
"There shall be no more pain" (Rev. 21:4).
Deaf . . . Blind . . . Lame . . . Healed (Isa. 35).

V. **A Place of Reunion.**
"Then . . . face to face" (1 Cor. 13:12).
"Many shall come from the east and west . . ." (Matt. 8:11).

SNAPPY SERMON STARTERS

THE "I WILLS" OF ISAIAH 41

I.   *"I will* strengthen thee" (v. 10).

II. *"I will* help thee" (v. 10). His promise is enough, because His presence is a fact.

III. *"I will* uphold thee" (v. 10). He sustains. His arms are underneath.

IV. *"I will* hold thy right hand" (v. 13). Help in service.

V.   "Fear not; *I will* help thee" (v. 13). He is our co-partner. See how God assures and reassures His timid child.

VI. "Fear not thou worm Jacob, *I will* help thee" (v. 14). "When I am weak, then am I strong" (2 Cor. 12:10). Here we see that God takes as an illustration the lowliest of His creatures as showing forth the littleness of the believer and the utter weakness of his strength.

VII. *"I will* make thee a sharp threshing instrument" (v. 15). His Word, too, is sharper than any two-edged sword (Heb. 4:12,13).

VIII. *"I will* hear them" (v. 17). "His ear is ever opened to their cry."

IX. *"I will* not forsake them" (v. 17). See Romans 8:38,39.

X.   *"I will* open rivers" (v. 18). Refreshment. He does not say "rivulets," "brooks," or "creeks," but *rivers*.

XI. *"I will* make the wilderness a pool of water" (v. 18). When a saint is filled with the Holy Spirit, the Gospel will spread like a mighty pool of water. His testimony will then have weight and influence.

XII. *"I will* plant in the wilderness" (v. 19). "And what the Lord plants the devil cannot pull up to destroy" (John 10:28).

XIII. *"I will* set" (v. 19). Blessed be God for full assurance and establishment in the truth (John 5:24).

J. E. WOLFE

WHAT DOES IT MEAN TO FOLLOW JESUS?

It is well that we should ponder the privileges of the Christian life, but we must not forget that those privileges mean corresponding responsibilities; and it is also well to remember that we cannot fulfill the responsibilities, only as we enjoy by faith the privileges. To come to Christ, and to receive from Christ, are our privileges; and to abide in Christ, and to follow after Him, are our responsibilities.

To follow Christ, means at least three things; and these are— sacrifice, suffering, and glory.

I. Sacrifice.

In the case of the disciples it meant leaving their nets (Matt. 4:19,20): with Matthew, forsaking the "receipt of custom" (Matt. 9:9); and with the rich young ruler it was "sell all that thou hast, and distribute to the poor" (Luke 18:22). To follow Christ, means at least two things, namely, the denial of self itself (Matt. 16:24); and putting Christ and His claims first (Luke 9:57-62).

II. Suffering.

Christ's distinct and definite command to Peter, as He tells him that he will have to die for Him, is, "Follow Me" (John 21:19). Peter understood that to mean death (1 Peter 1:14). There is a "cross" for every follower of Christ (Mark 10:21), and a death to the self-life, in order that we may bring forth fruit unto God (John 12:24-26). Jordan with its baptism, Gethesemane with its bitter cup, Gabbatha with its fiendish mockery, Golgotha with its shame, the Cross with its suffering, the darkness with its cry, and Calvary with its death, have their counterpart in our experience.

III. Glory.

It is to His followers that Christ promises that they shall "sit in the throne of His glory" (Matt. 19:28); who shall be with Him, and also be honored by the Father (John 12:26). Christ not only leads His followers to the Mount of Calvary to suffer with Him, but He also leads them to the Mount of Transfiguration, that they may be glorified with Him.

To follow Christ in holiness of life, in compassion of heart, in devotion of service, in abandonment of will, in patience of spirit, in earnestness of soul, and in loyalty to truth, is to evidence that we are His sheep (John 10:27). Surely, this is the least we can do, even as

Bartimaeus (Mark 10:52), and the noble band of women (Matt. 27:55). Of the former we read, "He followed Jesus in the way," and of the latter we read, "which followed Jesus into Galilee, ministering unto Him."

F. E. MARSH

THE PRESENCE OF JESUS

. . . Jesus went unto them, walking on the sea . . . (Matt. 14:25-33).

I.   The Problem of His Presence
"They were troubled." "They cried out for fear." They did not recognize Jesus. He is always present. He is with us always. We should always be able to recognize Him and be willing to honor Him everywhere.

II.   The Proof of His Presence
Jesus assured the disciples of His presence with the same clear voice that they had often heard. He said, "Be of good cheer; it is I; be not afraid." Hear the voice of Jesus who comes to us just when we need Him most.

III.   The Permission of His Presence
There was doubt in the heart of Peter, and Jesus gave him permission to walk on the water and to come to Him, but Peter's faith failed when he took his eyes off Jesus and saw the boisterous waves. Jesus is willing to be tried.

IV.   The Power of His Presence
When Peter began to sink, he cried unto Jesus, "Lord, save me." Jesus stretched forth His hand and lifted the disciple out of trouble and calmed the waves. Jesus has power to control nature. He has all power and will manifest it to save the people. Call on Him.

V.   The Praise of His Presence
"They that were in the ship came and worshipped Him, saying, Of a truth thou art the Son of God." Hearts of praise should be lifted to Jesus for all that He is to our weak and failing lives. Praise Him. Worship Him. Love Him. Live in the presence of Jesus and allow Him to give blessings.

SERMONS IN OUTLINE

ONCE

One of the key-words of Hebrews 9 and 10 is the term "once," which occurs seven times.

I. The Once of Limitation (9:7).

The High Priest could only enter the Holiest of all, one day in the year, though he went in several times on that one day.

II. The Once of Completion (9:12).

The Revised Version says that Christ has entered into the Holiest *"once for all"*; therefore, His atoning work is complete. Mark also the contrast—Christ entered in with His own blood.

III. The Once of Manifestation (9:26, R.V.).

Christ was hidden behind the veil of His Godhead before His incarnation, but He is God manifest in the flesh. Ponder the purpose of His appearing; it was to "put away sin," which sin kept man from God, and God from man.

IV. The Once of Condemnation (9:27).

Death on account of sin, and judgment for sin, are the common heritage "laid up" (R.V., margin) for the natural man.

V. The Once of Substitution (9:28).

Those who believe in Christ, and know Him personally as their Savior and Lord, are not looking for death or judgment, but for His second coming, because Christ has stood in their place and borne the judgment for them. Mark the *"as"* and *"so"* of 9:27,28.

VI. The Once of Purification (10:2).

The sacrifices under the Levitical system were only effectual in atoning for the sins of the past year, and did not cleanse the conscience; but Christ has, once and forever, dealt with the question of sin in its penal aspect. The believer is no longer a condemned criminal at the bar of justice, but a child in God's family, with a perfect conscience, and freed from guilt.

VII. The Once of Sanctification (10:10).

The blood of Christ, which is the purchase of our salvation, is also the means of our separation to God. As those who are sanctified in Christ to God, which is our privilege, we are responsible to be separate in heart and life to the Lord in all things. We do not seek to be saintly to become saints, but as saints we are to do those things that are consistent with our calling (1 Cor. 1:2—the words *"to be"* are in italics; Eph. 5:3).

F. E. MARSH

PEACE

Grace, mercy, and peace are the trio of Gospel blessings. Grace is love *planning to bless*, mercy is *love acting*, and peace is *love enjoyed*.

P– Purchased Peace. There are many who talk about "making their peace with God." This is an impossibility. Man can never make his peace with God; but there is something better, and that is, that Christ has made peace by the blood of His Cross. The purchase price of the peace of the Gospel is the blood of Christ (Col. 1:20).

E– Embodied Peace. "He is our Peace." It is not merely something from Christ, but Christ Himself, who is the believer's peace (Eph. 2:14). I remember an aged saint exclaiming to me once, "Oh, I wish I had peace!" I asked her, "Have you Christ?" "Oh, yes!" she replied. "Then you have peace, because you have Christ, for 'He is our Peace.'" If we sever blessing from Christ we shall never enjoy blessing, but if we see that we *have* every blessing in Christ (Eph. 1:3), and that Christ *is* every blessing, then we have blessing.

A– Abiding Peace. "My peace I give unto you" (John 14:27) is Christ's gift to His people. Whatever Christ gives must be like Himself, enduring and unfailing, for He is "the same yesterday, today, and forever" (Heb. 13:8). The things of this world pass away (1 John 2:17), but the things of the world to come are like the words of Christ (Matt. 24:35), they never pass away.

C– Complete Peace. The peace of God is perfect in its nature and perfect in its keeping (Isa. 26:3). Like a circle, it is complete in its character, and encircling in its embrace. To be complete in Christ (Col. 2:10) is to have a complete peace, because we are in a complete Savior.

E– Ennobling Peace. When the Lord Jesus has said peace to the sin-sick soul (Luke 7:50), and when the peace of God rules in the heart (Col. 3:15), through being anxious for nothing, prayerful in everything, and thankful for anything (Phil. 4:6,7), then in the quietness and calmness which are begotten by the Holy Spirit (Rom. 15:13) the life shall be calm as a river (Isa. 66:12), and the peace of God shall play upon the face (Acts 6:15).

F. E. MARSH

THE PURPOSE OF PRAISE

Bless the Lord, O my soul, and forget not all His benefits (Ps. 103:2).

I. It Is Praise to God

"Bless the Lord." The Lord gives life and sustains it. We live and move and have our life in Him. We should praise Him for all physical and spiritual blessings. The Lord is worthy of all praise from all the people in all the earth.

II. It Is Praise from the Soul

"O my soul." The praise uttered here comes from a full heart. It is the very expression of the soul. The praise expressed here is from all the faculties and powers of the being. It expresses all that can come from the intellect, the feeling and the will of a grateful personality. This praise is the voice of the sincere soul. Such praise will lift the soul into the very presence of God.

III. It Is Praise for Benefits

"Forget not all His benefits." Praise the Lord for all He does for us in the physical and the spiritual realms. Study the seven benefits of the Lord mentioned in Psalm 103:3-6. He forgives our sins and saves our souls and we become children of His. He is the Great Physician and can heal all the diseases of the body when it is in accord with His holy will. He preserves life, crowns with loving-kindness, supplies every good thing that life needs, and gives continually the strength we need. How gracious is the Lord! What benefits to have Him always! Praise Him! Bless His name!

SERMONS IN OUTLINE
JEROME O. WILLIAMS

SYMBOLS OF THE WORD

A Mirror to show us ourselves (James 1:23)
A Hammer to break the will (Jer. 23:29)
A Fire to melt the heart (Jer. 23:29)
A Sword to pierce the conscience (Heb. 4:12)
A Seed to quicken the soul (1 Peter 1:23)
A Laver to cleanse the way (Eph. 5:26)
A Light to show the path (Ps. 119:105)

500 BIBLE SUBJECTS

REGENERATION

A New Life from God. An Inward Working in the Soul.

Its Necessity (John 3:7; Gal. 6:15; Eph. 2:2)
Its Nature (John 3:5; 2 Cor. 5:17; Eph. 2:10; 4:24)
Its Agent (John 3:8; 6:63; 2 Cor. 3:6; Titus 3:5)
Its Instrument (1 Peter 1:23; James 1:18; John 5:24)
Its Means (1 John 5:1; Gal. 3:26; John 1:12-13)
Its Fruits (1 John 3:9; Rom. 6:22; 1 John 3:10)
Its Manifestation (1 John 5:1-2; 3:16)

500 BIBLE SUBJECTS

SANCTIFICATION

The word means "to set apart" or "to separate"

The Sanctification of Believers (1 Cor. 1:2; 2 Thess. 2:13; 1 Peter 1:3)

I. **Perfect and Once for All**—The Work of the Cross, the Result of the Sacrifice of Christ (1 Cor. 6:11; Acts 20:32; 26:18; Heb. 2:11)

II. **Progressive and Continuous**—The Work of the Spirit through the Word in the believer (1 Thess. 5:23; John 17:17)

Types and Illustrations—The Sabbath sanctified (Gen. 2:3); the First-Born "set apart" (Ex. 13:2); The Brazen Altar, the Holy Garments (Ex. 29:44; 28:2) and the Holy Mount (2 Peter 1:18) accounted "sacred" or "holy," not intrinsically, but "set apart" by the presence and for the service of God.

500 BIBLE SUBJECTS

SAINTS IN GOD'S HAND

. . . all His saints are in Thy hand (Deut. 33:3).

I. Who Are Saints?

They are children of God by regeneration. They are "Born of the Spirit," "Born again," "new creatures," "created in Christ Jesus unto good works."

II. Saints Are in God's Hand.

It may be said that all God's creatures are in His hand; but the saints are so in a peculiar sense. This will appear if we consider:

A. They are in His loving hand. His is the hand of a Father and surely He loves those whom He has made His children in so costly a manner, even through the incarnation and death of His own Son.

B. They are in His guiding hand. Well it is for them that they are not left to their own guidance. They know not the way in which they should go. They know not what is best for them.

C. They are in His protecting hand. How greatly they need protection! They need protection from themselves, protection from the evil influences of the world, and from the snares of Satan. His hand is stretched forth for their defense.

D. They are in His chastening hand. He chastens them with the paternal reluctance exemplified in a wise earthly father (Lam. 3:33). His love prompts the application of the chastening rod (Heb. 12:5-11).

E. They are in His sustaining hand. He holds them up, otherwise they would sink beneath the waves of sorrow. The hour of death comes apace. How greatly will they need divine support in that hour when all human helpers fail!

NOTES OF SERMONS

SEVEN-FOLD PRIVILEGES OF THE CHILD OF GOD

Saved (Deut. 33:29)
Secured (Deut. 33:3)
Separated (Deut. 33:16)
Satisfied (Deut. 33:23)
Sheltered (Deut. 33:29)
Seated (Deut. 33:3)
Sacrificing (Deut. 33:19)   Pegs for Preachers

THE FOUR PILLARS OF OUR SALVATION

Who is he that condemneth? It is Christ that died, yea rather, that is risen again, who also maketh intercession for us (Rom. 8:34).

I. The Four Fundamental Pillars of Our Salvation
   A. *Christ died for us*—His death was:
      1. Voluntary (John 15:13).
      2. Fearful and terrible (Matt. 27:34-53).
      3. Substitutionary (1 Peter 3:18).
   B. *He "is risen again."*
      1. He rose by His own power.
      2. He rose for our justification (Rom. 4:25).
      3. He is the first fruits of them who slept (1 Cor. 15:20).
   C. *He ascended to "the right hand of God."*
      1. Visibly (Acts 1:9-11).
      2. Exercising dominion and kingly power over heaven, earth and hell (Phil. 2:9-11).
      3. To send down the gift of the Holy Ghost (John 16:7).
   D. *He intercedes for us* (1 John 2:1; Heb. 7:25; 9:24).

II. The Comfort the Believer Derives from These Truths
   Who is he that condemneth?
   A. *Our hearts cannot condemn us* (Rom. 8:1).
   B. *The world cannot condemn us* (Rom. 8:33; 4:25).
   C. *The devil cannot condemn us*—He is "the accuser of the brethren," but Christ ascended on high and now exercises kingly power over the devil.
   D. *The Father will not condemn us*—Christ is our Advocate. Happy state, to be forgiven!

100 Sermon Outlines

VICTORY

More than conquerors (Rom. 8:37).

The key-note of our text is "Victory." It is the characteristic of all God's works, that whatever He does, He does abundantly. There is always something in excess; a David's cup that runneth over, or a Joseph's bough which runneth over the wall.

Every miracle was done overflowingly. The lame man not only walked but leaped. When the daughter of Jairus was raised to life, Jesus commands that "something be given her to eat"; and the very fragments of His feedings are "twelve baskets full."

Christ came to this world "that we might have life, more abundantly."The life in union with Him is a truer and a greater life than unfallen life, than any angel's life could ever have been. "We are more than conquerors."

I. **Consider How Christ Was "More Than Conqueror."**
    A. In His death.
        1. A prayer for His enemies.
        2. A provision of filial tenderness for His mother.
        3. A free pardon to a sinner.
        4. The generosity of a kingdom with a royal hand.
        5. These were the achievements of the dying man, Christ Jesus. "More than conqueror."

    B. In His rising.
        1. The victory would have been complete if that body had come forth the same, but He did more.
        2. The body was more beautiful, more spiritual than the body which was laid in the grave.

    C. In His ascension and exaltation.
        1. He ascends but does not leave His followers to weep—for He is more with them than before—He is exalted, and none are orphaned. He is "more than conqueror."

II. **The Believer Is "More Than Conqueror."**
    A. In the contest with Satan, God undertakes that His people shall not be overcome, and more, that they shall overcome the enemy and put him to flight. "He will flee from you."

B.   Then a sin overcome necessarily becomes a virtue.

    1.   Satan is foiled with his own weapons, and Israel enriched with the spoils of Egypt.

    2.   That too much speaking will become eloquence for Christ, that temper will make zeal.

C.   The Christian would not exchange the dark memories of sorrow and bereavement for the sunniest of the world's hours.

    1.   There was so much of Christ in them, so much of a tranquil mind, so much of heaven, that he comes out of the sorrow "more than conqueror."

    2.   And so when we die, like a ship, at high tide, pressing full-sailed into port, "an entrance is ministered unto us abundantly" into the kingdom. The world may conquer—the church is "more than conqueror."

SELECTED